How to make simple wooden
PUZZLES &
JIGSAWS

Alan, Gill and Glyn Bridgewater

SEARCH PRESS

First published in Great Britain 1993
Search Press Limited
Wellwood, North Farm Road,
Tunbridge Wells, Kent TN2 3DR

ISBN 0 85532 759 6

Acknowledgements
We would like to thank the following individuals for their
assistance: Tracy A. Emmison of Humbrol Paints; Glen Tizard of
Draper Tools Ltd.; Roger Buse of Hegner UK Ltd.; Cays Thomas
of Peter Pan Playthings, Harbutt's *Plasticine*; and Steven Morran
of Loctite UK.

If you have difficulty in obtaining any of the equipment or
materials mentioned in this book, please write for further
information to the Publishers: Search Press Ltd., Wellwood,
North Farm Road, Tunbridge Wells, Kent TN2 3DR.

Dedication
*Dedicated to Geoff Newsham and Martin Grimley.
Thanks for seeing me through that dreaded bookcase
project. If it wasn't for your help, I would still be
messing around with bits of veneer – that goes for you,
too, J.K.M. and S.A.H.*

Printed in Spain by A.G. Elkar S. Coop, 48012 Bilbao.

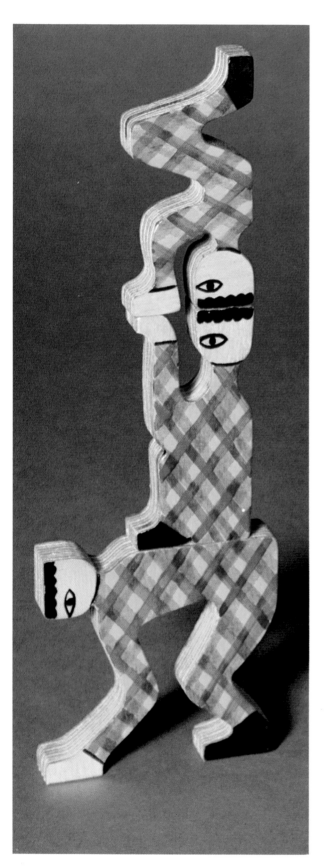

Contents

Introduction

Most of us, children and adults alike, enjoy the challenge of puzzles, from five-thousand-piece jigsaws to fiendish little wooden-block puzzles – they are all good fun. But why do we find puzzles so irresistible? I think the truth is that we all like problem-solving, and what is particularly satisfying about a puzzle is that it has a definite clear-cut no-argument solution. There is no question of 'perhaps' or 'maybe' – when we are dealing with puzzles, gratification is guaranteed!

The first jigsaws, known as 'dissections' or 'dissected puzzles', were made in the late eighteenth century. Early examples were usually maps mounted on wood, with the various countries, regions and counties fretted out as separate pieces. The name 'jigsaw' comes either from the up-and-down action of the saw or from the template, pattern or 'jig' that was traditionally used in the sawing process.

There are eight projects in this book, ranging from traditional interlocking picture puzzles to original construction and cube puzzles. What child could resist a herd of elephants that link trunk-to-tail, or a bony dinosaur that nestles in its own 'excavation'? There is a set of Victorian gymnasts that can stack and balance on each other in the most amazing way, a mysterious jigsaw that interlocks to create a family of cats, and a panda picture scene – all in specially designed frames. For the more serious-minded, there is the nineteenth-century tangram puzzle, beautifully contained in its own special box: from its seven brilliantly coloured geometric shapes you can make any number of intriguing configurations and pictures. Finally, to torment the unsuspecting quite unmercifully, there is a tiny cube puzzle that is easy to take apart, but fiendishly difficult to put back together again.

Each project has been carefully set out, with detailed text, scaled drawings, step-by-step hands-on illustrations and captions to guide you through every stage. All measurements are listed in millimetres as well as in inches. There is also a comprehensive A-Z of primary puzzle-making tools, materials and techniques. A wide range of tools and techniques is used, the idea being that you can study the possibilities and then choose the approach that suits you best. So for example, although we use a variety of saws – ranging from electric scroll saws to less expensive hand tools like the fretsaw, coping saw and piercing saw – you can modify the project to suit your own tool kit.

Whether you are an experienced woodworker or a complete novice, as long as you like the notion of puzzles, then this is the book for you.

Tools, materials and techniques

You might like to look at the comprehensive list at the back of this book before you start your first puzzle, especially if you are new to puzzle-making or need guidance in buying tools and materials.

Traditional jigsaw puzzle (instructions on page 6) – a picture made up of interlocking flatwood pieces.

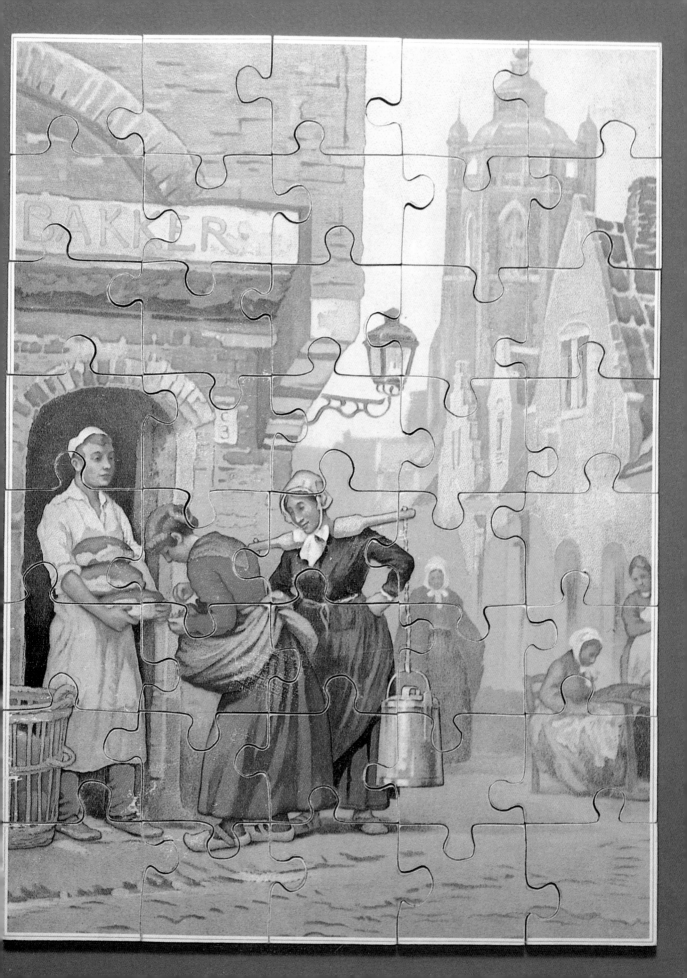

Traditional jigsaw puzzle

About the puzzle

The jigsaw measures 204 x 280mm (8 x 11in) and is based on a grid of 38 x 38mm (1½ x 1½ in), with the cut-outs running in straight lines vertically and horizontally across the puzzle (fig. 1.1 on page 7).

The picture, taken from a give-away baker's calendar, is mounted directly on to a sheet of 6mm (¼ in) thick birch-faced plywood, and the individual pieces are cut out with a fretsaw.

Making the puzzle

Choosing a print

When you are choosing a print, it is best to go for a subject that contains a lot of detail and visual texture. For a jigsaw, it is important that the spread of detail/texture is such that just about every piece within the puzzle is linked visually with its neighbour. For instance, in terms of artistic appreciation you might well prefer a Toulouse-Lautrec print, with its wonderful lines and beautiful areas of flat colour, to a florid chocolate-box Landseer, but how would you relate the puzzle pieces one to another if they contained nothing more than flat colour?

Mounting the print

Run an inch or so of water in the bath, then take the jigsaw print and carefully slide it into the water. Let it soak and stretch for about five minutes – if not soaked properly, it will wrinkle. Meanwhile, clear the work surface of clutter, make sure that the plywood is clean and in good condition, and see that all the tools and materials are close to hand.

Check that the working surface of the plywood is completely free from dust and debris, mix a small amount of white water-soluble PVA glue with water, and give the face of the wood a couple of coats. The glue–water mix should be smooth and runny like single cream.

Take the print out of the water, set it face down on a clean wipe-dry surface like a kitchen worktop, and give it a couple of generous coats of the glue–water mix. Then carefully peel up the print and carefully lower it down in position on the plywood

(fig. 1.2 – top). Make sure it is well aligned and then gently ease away any trapped pockets of air by running the brush from centre to side and backwards and forwards across the print (fig. 1.2 – bottom). Be careful not to crease it!

When the print is nicely in position, give the face a couple of coats of the glue–water mix and put everything on one side to dry. With PVA glue it does not matter if you get glue on the face of the work, because it dries clear.

Fig. 1.2

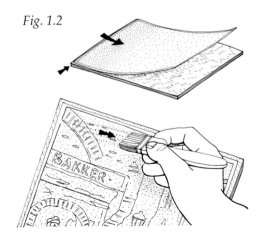

Fig. 1.1 - the jigsaw design: the scale is four grid squares to 25mm (1in).

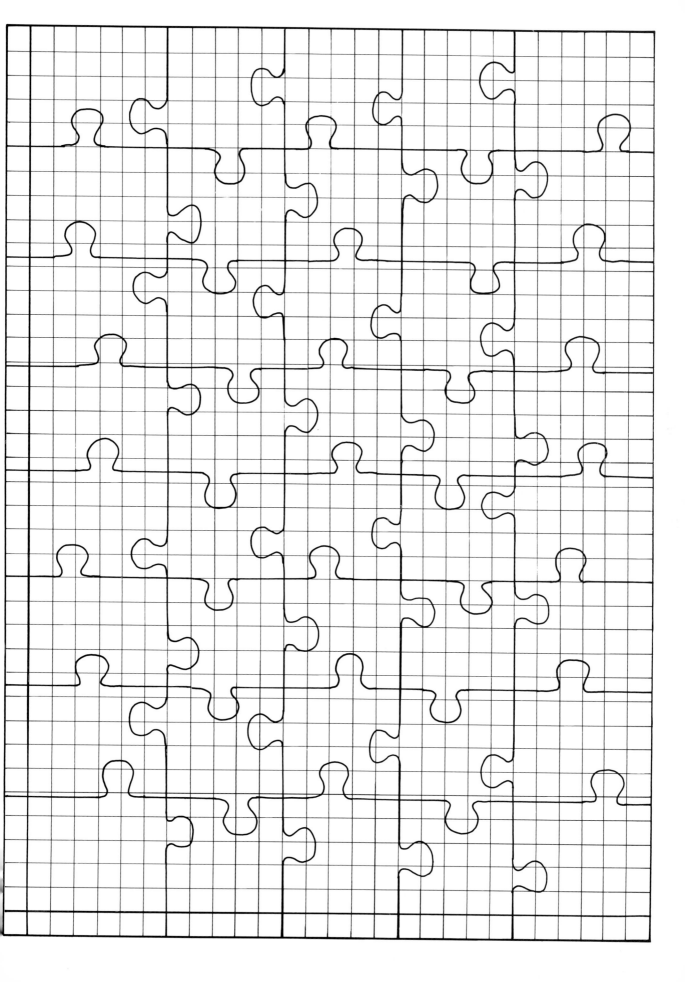

Drawing out the design

Look at our working drawing and note how, because of the nature of the interlocking tongue-and-mouth jigsaw design, it is possible to cover a large puzzle simply by repeating and linking two grids. So to make a longer or wider puzzle, just link and repeat the grid side-by-side or end-to-end so as to run the grid lines off the sides of your print. Draw the print size on your tracing paper and carefully, using the scaled grid as a guide, fill in the interlocking jigsaw design. Then lay the tracing, pencil side down, on the print, make sure that it is squarely aligned, and hinge it along the top edge with a strip of masking tape.

With a hard pencil and a ruler, painstakingly trace the grid design through to the face of the print (fig. 1.3). It is best to transfer all the little tongues, and then link them up with ruled lines. From time to time throughout the transferring process, hinge the tracing paper back and make sure that the grid lines are well established. It does not matter if you have an impressed line rather than a pencil line, as long as you can see it.

Fig. 1.3

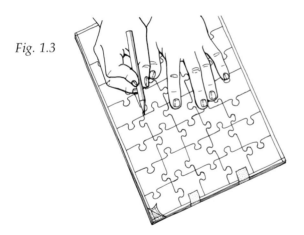

Fretsawing and finishing

Take away the tracing and remove the work-piece to the cutting area: now for the long and tricky task of fretting out the puzzle. With a new blade fitted and well tensioned in the saw frame so that the teeth point downwards (so any rough edges will appear underneath the print), set the board face-up on the edge of the bench and saw away the waste margin from around the print.

With the work held and manoeuvred in one hand and the saw operated with the other, slowly and methodically run the line of cut along the drawn line. Now, still with the print-side uppermost,

Fig. 1.4

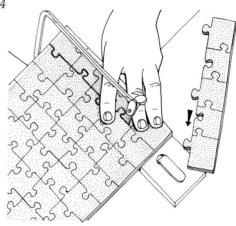

carefully cut the board down into strips (fig. 1.4). It is all pretty straightforward, as long as you hold the saw so that the blade runs through the wood at right angles to the sawn face, and as long as you work at a steady, even rate. When using a fretsaw, the rate of cut is best thought of as the up-and-down speed of the saw blade in relation to the forward pressure on the saw and the consequent speed of cut. I like to keep up a fast blade movement and a small amount of forward pressure on the saw. Certainly this way of working makes for slow going, but then again the sawn edge is so clean and sharp that it needs a minimum of sanding.

Continue cutting the board down into strips, and then cut the strips down into individual pieces (fig. 1.5). Finally, fret out all the pieces and rub the edges down with fine sandpaper, taking care not to snag the surface of the print.

The finished puzzle is illustrated on page 5.

Fig. 1.5

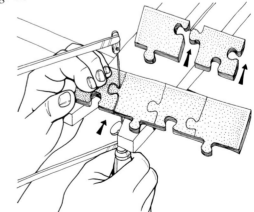

Pete the pentaceratops puzzle

About the puzzle

Have a look at the working drawing on page 10 (fig. 2.1) and see how, at the scale of four grid squares to 25mm (1in), the jigsaw puzzle measures 225 x 150mm (9 x 6in). Study the design templates on page 11 (figs. 2.2 and 2.3).

The puzzle is made up from three layers – a bottom board, the fretted and pierced middle puzzle-piece layer, and the top board or lid. Consider how the layers are fixed and organised in such a way that the puzzle pieces are contained and held in place by the lid being located on four turn-buttons. Study the details and see the way each turn-button is made up from two identical round-ended cut-outs, these being a spacer that is glue-fitted direct to the puzzle layer, and also the actual turn-button itself, which is screw-fitted on top of

Tools and materials

A sheet of best-quality white-faced 6mm ($\frac{1}{4}$in) thick multi-core plywood at about 600 x 300mm (24 x 12in) (this allows for various cutting arrangements and for waste) • four 22mm ($\frac{7}{8}$in) long brass round-head screws, with eight brass washers to fit • white PVA wood glue • double-sided tape • four small pots/cans of model-makers' transparent cellulose paint in red, yellow, blue and green • cellulose thinner to clean the brushes • clear high-gloss varnish • a sheet each of workout and tracing paper • pencil, ruler and compass • an electric scroll-saw • a large flat-bladed cross-cut saw • a hand drill with a 4mm ($\frac{1}{8}$in) diameter bit • a pack of graded sand-papers • two soft-haired paintbrushes (a broad point and a fine point).

A boxed dinosaur inlay toy.

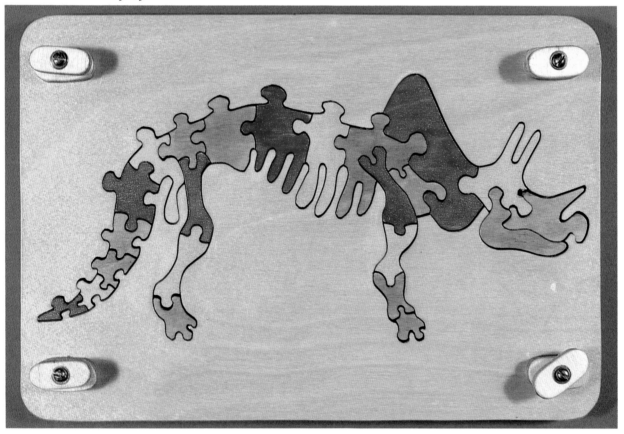

the spacer, so that its under-side is flush with the top of the lid.

The design is particularly interesting in that the puzzle pieces are not only bone-like in shape, but are also painted in a red, yellow, blue and green colour sequence. The lid can be carefully removed, the pieces can be spread out and grouped according to colour, type and size, and then all the little bones, ribs and vertebrae can be slotted back together again. Good quiet fun!

Bearing in mind that many of the puzzle pieces are small, though, I think it fair to say that this is not a suitable toy for toy-sucking toddlers.

Making the puzzle

Setting out the wood, designing and tracing

Take a pencil and ruler, and set the plywood out so that you have three boards at 175 x 250mm (7 x 10in). This measurement allows for cutting wastage of 13mm (½in) and results in a finished puzzle size of 150 x 225mm (6 x 9in).

Draw your chosen grid on the workout paper, and then copy the lines of the design one square at a time. So, for example, if you want to stay with the 'four grid squares to 25mm (1in)' scale and have a finished puzzle size of 150 x 225mm (6 x 9in), all you do is draw out a full-size grid – whereby four squares really do measure 25mm (1in) – and then transfer our design square by square (fig. 2.1).

When you have achieved a good full-size design drawing, take a 2B pencil, a ruler and a sheet of tracing paper, and make a careful tracing.

Cutting the boards, drilling the turn-button holes and tracing the design

When you have set the sheet of plywood out – so that you have three 175 x 250mm (7 x 10in) boards and a couple of strips of waste – take the large flat-bladed saw and swiftly slice the wood down. Stack the three boards in this order from top to bottom – the turn-button-hole board, the dinosaur outline board, and the base board – and sandwich them securely together with strips of double-sided tape between all mating layers. Then take the pencil,

Fig. 2.1 – working drawing/painting grid showing puzzle layer.

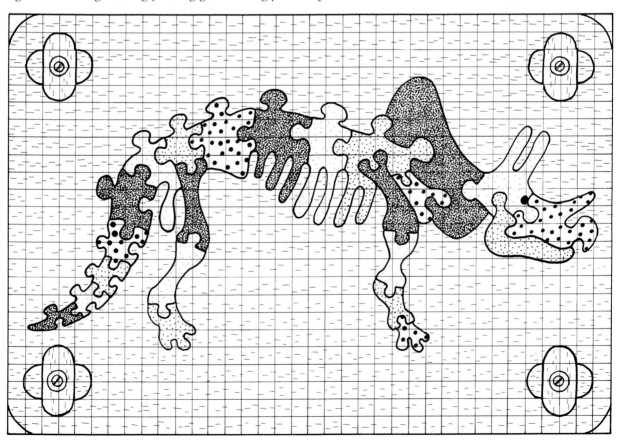

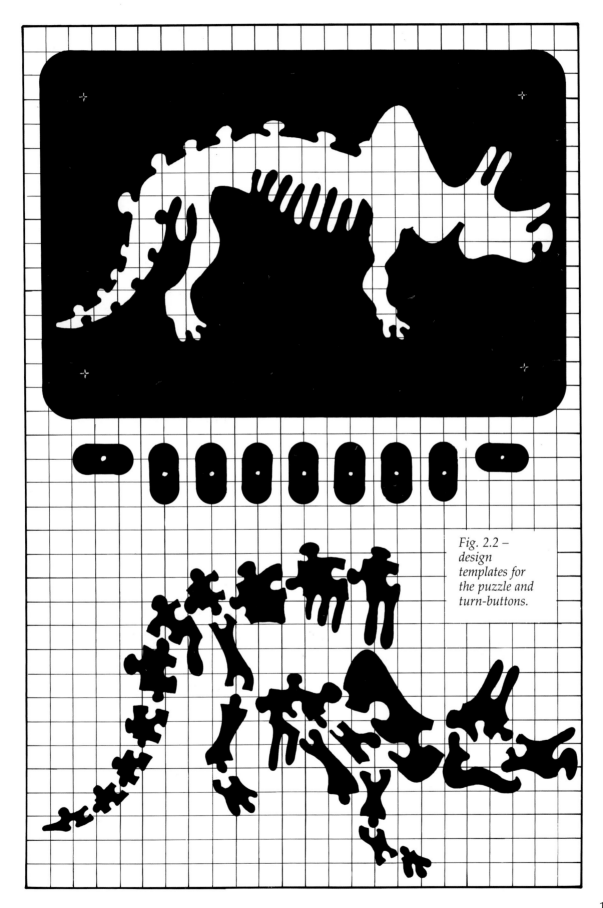

Fig. 2.2 – design templates for the puzzle and turn-buttons.

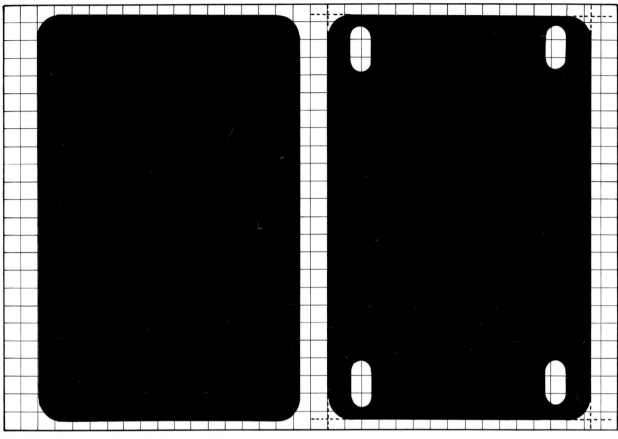

Fig. 2.3 – design templates for the top and bottom layers.

ruler and compass and make sure that the round-cornered board profile is nicely and precisely established. If all is well, each of the four corners should be set out with a 13mm (½in) diameter radius curve, the overall puzzle should measure 150 x 225mm (6 x 9in), and there should be an all-round strip of waste at about 13mm (½in) wide (fig. 2.4 – top).

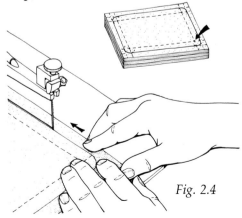

Fig. 2.4

When you are happy with the way the wood is set out, move the scroll saw and set to work cutting out the round-cornered shape. With the saw table clean and, better still, slightly wax-polished, and with the saw blade well tensioned, switch on the power and run the wood through the saw.

When using the scroll saw, be sure to hold the work firmly against the table, otherwise the action of the blade will whip the piece out of your hands. Also remember that to follow a curve you must rotate the work-piece rather than push against the side of the blade. As long as the line of cut is slightly to the waste side of the drawn line, you should end up with pieces of the size and shape you intended and which fit together (fig. 2.4 – bottom).

When you have achieved the round-cornered shape, pencil-label the board edges 'top', 'middle' and 'bottom' – meaning the three layers within the sandwich – and pencil a couple of registration marks across the cut edges. When you have done this, very carefully ease off the 'bottom' board and put it to one side. Now mark in the position of the

12

turn-button centres and drill them through with a 4mm ($\frac{1}{8}$ in) bit (fig. 2.5 – left).

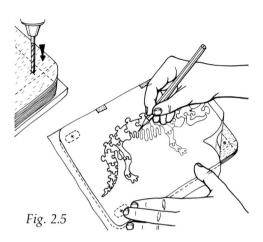

Fig. 2.5

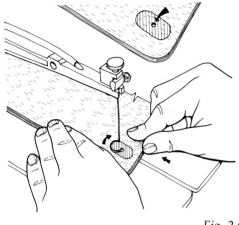

Fig. 2.6

Finally, ease the two boards apart and remove all traces of adhesive tape.

Now, starting with the top board or lid, secure the tracing with tabs of masking tape, and use a hard 3H pencil to trace the top board turn-button-hole details through to the working face of the wood (see fig. 2.2 on page 11), i.e. carefully rework the back of the traced lines so that the graphite from the tracing impresses itself through to the wood. Repeat the procedure with a second board, only this time concentrate your efforts on the shape of the dinosaur puzzle-pieces. It is all easy enough as long as you use a hard pencil for pressing (fig. 2.5 – right). Along the way, hinge the tracing back and check that all is correct. If necessary, go over any fuzzy lines.

Finally, pin all the drawings and tracings up on the wall so that they are out of harm's way, but within easy reach.

Fretting the turn-button holes and the puzzle pieces

Take the 'top' board back to the scroll saw. Bearing in mind that this stage is tricky and that you only have one shot at getting it right, unhitch the blade, pass it through one or other of the drilled turn-button screw/pilot holes (fig. 2.6 – top), refit the blade, adjust the tension, and then very carefully cut out the little round-ended turn-button hole (fig. 2.6 – bottom). You will not go far wrong as long as you go at an easy pace.

Keep the wood moving so that the saw blade is presented with the line of cut, and see to it that the cut line is a little to the waste side of the drawn line.

Carry on cutting out one hole, unhitching the blade, and then on to the next hole, until all four holes have been cut. If you are a beginner, have a try-out on some scrap wood first.

Take the 'middle' board, check that the transferred dinosaur puzzle outline is correctly aligned with the turn-button screw holes and the edge of the board, and then drill out the single pilot 'eye' hole. Have a look at the working drawing on page 10 (fig. 2.1) and see how the 'eye' is shown as a black dot. Having done this, move back to the scroll saw, unhitch the blade, pass it through the pilot hole, refit and retension the blade, and then cut out all the pieces that go to make up the puzzle. This stage is not too difficult, because it is not a problem if the cut line wavers slightly off the drawn line. Be careful not to cut the little puzzle-piece link-necks too narrow.

When you have cut out all the puzzle pieces, take a piece of scrap ply and cut out the eight little round-ended turn-button shapes. Check that the cut-outs fit the top-board holes, and cut a few more than you need. Select the best eight to make the four matched pairs and drill out the centres in readiness for the screws.

Putting it all together

You should now have: a plain bottom board, a middle board with the puzzle pieces fretted out and with drilled turn-button screw holes, a top board with the turn-button holes fretted out, and eight turn-button shapes. If necessary, fill damaged areas and rub down with the graded sandpapers until all surfaces are smooth to the touch.

Take the bottom and middle boards, smear a

small amount of glue on mating surfaces, and set them together so that the registration marks are aligned. Set the top board in place, and then strap the whole sandwich up with masking tape.

Take the eight turn-button shapes, and set them out so that there are two cut-outs for each hole – a spacer-pillar piece that is going to be glued on to the middle puzzle-piece board, and the actual turn-button.

Take the spacer, smear a small amount of glue on the mating surface, and set it in place in its allotted hole (fig. 2.7 – top). Make sure that the spacer is a well-centred fit, and then screw the turn-button in place on top of the spacer (fig. 2.7 – bottom).

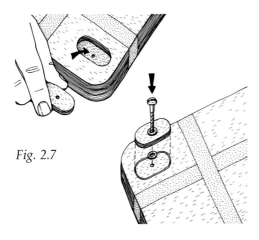

Fig. 2.7

Just for the moment, turn the screw hard down on its washers until the button is a good tight immovable fit. Do this with all four turn-buttons. Remove the lid and use a damp cloth to wipe away all excess glue from around the turn-button spacers and from the puzzle-piece cavity. When the glue is dry, remove the screws and the four turn-buttons in readiness for painting.

Painting and finishing

Wipe away all the dust and debris and remove the work-piece to the area set aside for painting. Study the painting grid (fig. 2.1). Bearing in mind that only the top face of each puzzle piece is to be painted and that you are only going to use four colours in the sequence red, yellow, blue and green, set the puzzle pieces face up and in order on the work surface and pencil-label each piece. Starting at the tail end with red, work in sequence along the body and through to the head: red, yellow, blue, green, and so on, until you finish up with the nose being labelled green.

When you come to the leg pieces, start with red

and continue the sequence down the leg. When all the pieces have been labelled, group them in colours and paint the top surface of each piece (fig. 2.8 – top). The best procedure is to hold the puzzle piece in one hand and the loaded brush in the other, then to place the tip of the brush at the centre of the piece and to draw it across the surface and towards the edge. As the brush reaches the edge, lift it up and away in a continuous swift movement (fig. 2.8 – bottom). Try not to get paint on any of the sawn edges.

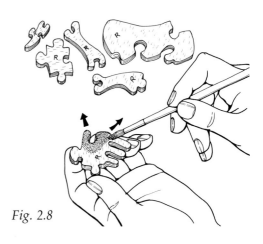

Fig. 2.8

When the paint is completely dry, and remembering to rub down with fine sandpaper between coats, give the whole work-piece a couple of coats of thin clear varnish. To complete the puzzle, place washers either side of the turn-button, then screw the turn-buttons in place so that they are an easy-to-move fit.

Useful advice

When you are pencil-press-transferring, be sure to use a soft 2B pencil for the initial tracing and a hard 3H pencil for the pressing. If you have a choice, use best-quality heavy-duty tracing paper. Although you can transfer the design by means of a sheet of carbon paper, I prefer to use the pencil-press method because I find that carbon tends to smear and be rather messy. If you are not so happy with using the grid method to draw the design up to size, you could use a photocopier instead.

If you use cellulose paints, be sure to match the paint-type up with an appropriate thinner. Be warned – if you use the wrong type the brushes will be ruined.

Bearing in mind that a build-up of varnish on the edges of the pieces could result in an impossible-to-use tight-wedge fit, apply the varnish in thin coats.

Tangram puzzle

About the puzzle

Traditionally, tangrams were considered to be delicate and valuable items. They were sometimes made from ivory and decorated with intricate filigree designs, and all the pieces fitted in a little box. This tangram is boxed, too, and each piece is stained a different colour. If you would rather not go to the trouble of making a box, just cut out the pieces from one square of wood and enjoy playing with the puzzle.

The box, in the form of a sleeve, contains a shallow square tray into which the tangram pieces are arranged. The working drawing on page 16 shows how, at a scale of four grid squares to 25mm (1in), the puzzle measures 163mm (6½in) long and 150mm

Tangram – a traditional set of geometric shapes contained in a wooden sleeve.

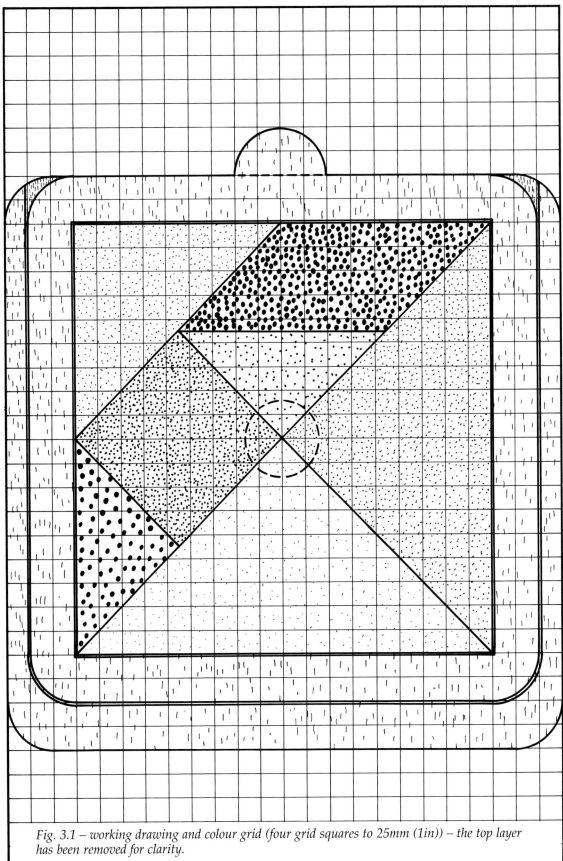

Fig. 3.1 – working drawing and colour grid (four grid squares to 25mm (1in)) – the top layer has been removed for clarity.

16

Tools and materials

Four sheets of best-quality 4mm (⅛ in) thick, white-faced multi-core plywood at 175 x 163mm (7 x 6½ in) (this allows for a small amount of cutting waste) • HB and 2B pencils • ruler • compass • set-square • a sheet of A4 (11¾ x 8¼ in) tracing paper • a coping saw and a few fine blades • a cross-cut saw • double-sided tape • a small amount of PVA glue • an electric drill and a 19mm (¾ in) diameter flatbit or hole saw, or alternatively a drill brace and a 19mm (¾ in) diameter auger bit • a hand drill and a 1.5mm (1⁄16 in) diameter bit • a small pin hammer • a handful of 6mm (¼ in) brass pins • a handful of 10mm (⅜ in) brass pins • a pack of graded sandpapers • brightly coloured water-based inks in red, orange, yellow, light green, dark green, dark blue and purple (water-based felt-tip markers can be used instead) • a No. 6 brush for applying the ink • a small quantity of natural furniture wax • a soft cotton rag for applying the wax and polishing.

(6in) wide (fig. 3.1). Study the design templates below and see how the box is constructed from four laminations of plywood and the way the tray and the tangram itself are both cut from the two centre layers (figs. 3.2 and 3.3). The hole detail in either side of the box shows which way up the tray is inside – otherwise the tray could be pulled out upside down and then all the pieces would fall out. The half-round finger-pull makes it easy to slide the tray in and out of the box.

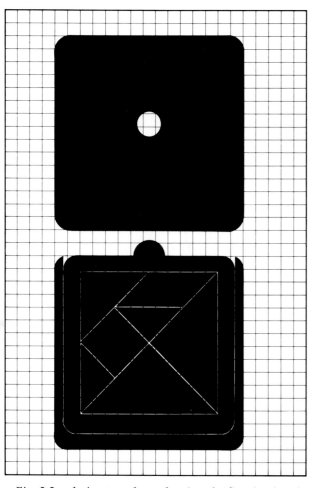

Fig. 3.2 – design templates showing the first (top) and second layers of the puzzle: the scale is five grid squares to 50mm (2in).

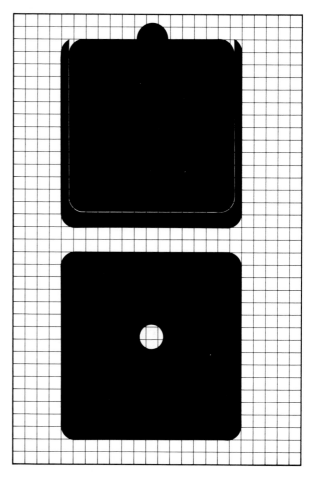

Fig. 3.3 – design templates showing the third and fourth (back or base) layers of the puzzle: the scale is five grid squares to 50mm (2in).

Making the puzzle

Setting out the design

Make a full-size drawing of the puzzle – refer to the working drawing and the design templates on pages 16 and 17 for all the details – and make a nice accurate tracing. Use a 2B pencil to go over all the lines on the reverse side of the tracing. Select the areas of plywood required. No part of this puzzle is covered up by layers of paint, so choose only the best wood: avoid filled areas, cavities, torn grain, splits and discoloured veneer.

Mark out four rectangles 175 x 163mm (7 x 6½ in) – there is no need to be too accurate – and cut each one out with a cross-cut saw. Use rough sandpaper to scuff away loose fibres left by the saw, and then stick all four layers together with double-sided tape. Select one side of the four-board sandwich to be 'top'. Use the pencil, compass and ruler to draw out the overall shape of the box, including the half-round finger-pull.

Cutting out

Set up the coping saw for cutting at 90° to the frame; rotate the swivelling spigots at each end of the frame so that the saw teeth point sideways, and tension the blade by twisting the handle. Hold the four-board sandwich so that part of it overhangs the edge of a work surface, and begin sawing out the shape, cutting to the waste side of the pencil line (fig. 3.4 – left).

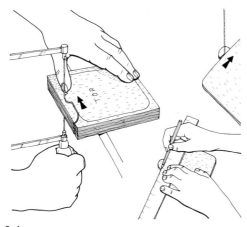

Fig. 3.4

Sawing through the four-board thickness is hard work, but it cannot be rushed. Keep the saw nice and steady and try to maintain even strokes; it is only too easy to wobble off course, break a blade, or cut crookedly through the thickness of the wood.

Once you have completed the cut, scribble a registration mark on the side of the sandwich. Prise off just the top layer and the base or bottom layer and remove the double-sided tape. The half-round finger-pull shapes are not needed on these pieces, so mark a straight line across each and saw them off (fig. 3.4 – right). Use the tracing to mark the centre of the 19mm (¾ in) diameter hole in each piece.

Whether you use an electric drill and a flatbit or holesaw, or a drill brace and an auger bit, you will need to clamp the work-piece firmly to a surface – if you do not have a clamp, get someone to hold the work-piece for you. Have a piece of waste wood underneath the hole so that the drill bit does not damage the work surface. Take up the middle two pieces which are still sandwiched together, and attach the tracing to the top surface. Transfer all the details of the frame and tangram pieces, remove the tracing, and check that all the lines are clear. Note that it is extremely important to confirm the accuracy of the tangram pieces using a set-square and ruler.

Use the coping saw to separate the square tray shape from the surrounding frame (fig. 3.5 – left).

Fig. 3.5

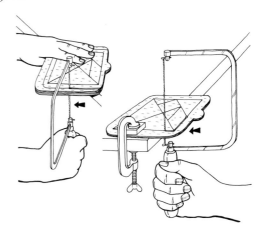

Keep the rounded-off corners nice and even. Scribble a registration mark on the edge of the sandwich, prise the two square tray shapes apart and put aside the bottom one. On the square with the tangram marked out on it, drill a 1.5mm (¹⁄₁₆ in) hole for entering a saw blade. A hole drilled at a junction, rather than in the middle of a line, is less noticeable. Unhitch the blade from the coping saw frame, pass it through the hole, rehitch the blade, and finally tension the blade. Let the work-piece overhang the surface, and cut along the pencil lines to separate all the tangram pieces (fig. 3.5 – right).

Assembling, staining and waxing

Sand every part of the puzzle to a good finish. Concentrate on edges – try using sandpaper wrapped around a flat stick of wood for this – and soften the sharp corners of the tangram pieces using sandpaper wrapped around a wooden block. When everything is smooth, take up the base and the frame that go to make up the square tray. Practise lining up the scribbled registration mark, and check that the sides are flush (fig. 3.6 – left).

Fig. 3.6

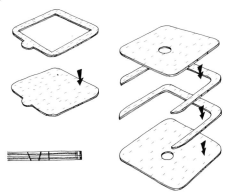

When you are satisfied, place the tray parts upside down on a sturdy work surface, and spread a thin film of glue all over the under-side of the frame part. Position the base correctly and hammer in about eight equally spaced 6mm (¹/₄ in) brass pins. If the pins threaten to break through the top surface, remove their heads with a pair of pliers. Remove any excess glue with a clean damp cloth.

Practise assembling the parts which make up the box: as long as you line up the scribbled registration mark and then check all the edges are flush, the tray is guaranteed to fit into the box perfectly (fig. 3.6 – right). Have some 10mm (³/₈ in) brass pins to hand, and then spread a thin film of glue over both faces of each narrow frame.

Put the layers together in the right order and then hold the sandwich together with short strips of masking tape. Hammer about seven pins in one side, equally spaced around the three edges that need fixing, then turn the box over and insert another seven pins, making sure that no pin is

directly opposite to one on the other side. Again, any glue that is squeezed out can be wiped away with a damp cloth once the tape has been removed. If you discover that the edges are a little uneven – perhaps due to a piece moving out of position fractionally – they can be smoothed out with sandpaper wrapped round a wooden block. Go over every part of the puzzle, smoothing faces and edges and rounding off corners with fine sandpaper. Put all the tangram parts in the square recess in the tray and slide it into the box. It should be a nice fit.

Take each piece of the tangram puzzle, one at a time, refer to the working drawing and colour grid, and then apply the water-based ink. For a nice even density of colour it is best to start by staining the edges, and then finish by covering both sides; start at the furthest edge and, while working towards yourself, streak the ink from side to side. A second coat will even out any light and dark patches.

Finish up by coating every part of the puzzle – except the inside of the box – with a layer of furniture wax. Rub the wax into the wood with a clean cotton rag, let it harden, and then buff it up with a different part of the rag. The wood soaks up the wax, which brings out the grain, enhances the colours and gives the pieces a beautiful semi-matt surface (and a pleasant smell as well!). Later on, a second coat of wax might be needed.

When all is complete, why not try recreating some of the tangram configurations shown in fig. 3.7? (See page 20). Remember, all seven shapes must be used and no shape should overlap another!

Useful advice

There is no reason to stain the tangram pieces in the colours we have suggested. If your own inks happen to be a different range of colours, why not try out alternative combinations?

If you do not have either type of drill or a 19mm (³/₄ in) diameter drill bit, you could cut out the hole details with a coping saw. Start by marking out a 19mm (³/₄ in) diameter circle with a compass, and then drill a small starting hole for the saw blade. Enter the blade through the hole, retension the frame, and cut out the best circle you can manage. Wrap sandpaper around a dowel and sand out any irregularities.

The tangram puzzle would look nice displayed on a wall. You need only make the tray part of the project, and alter the design slightly; make the tangram pieces twice as thick – so the pieces do not fall out of the frame – and drill a key-hole shape in the half-round finger-pull so that it can be hung up on a nail.

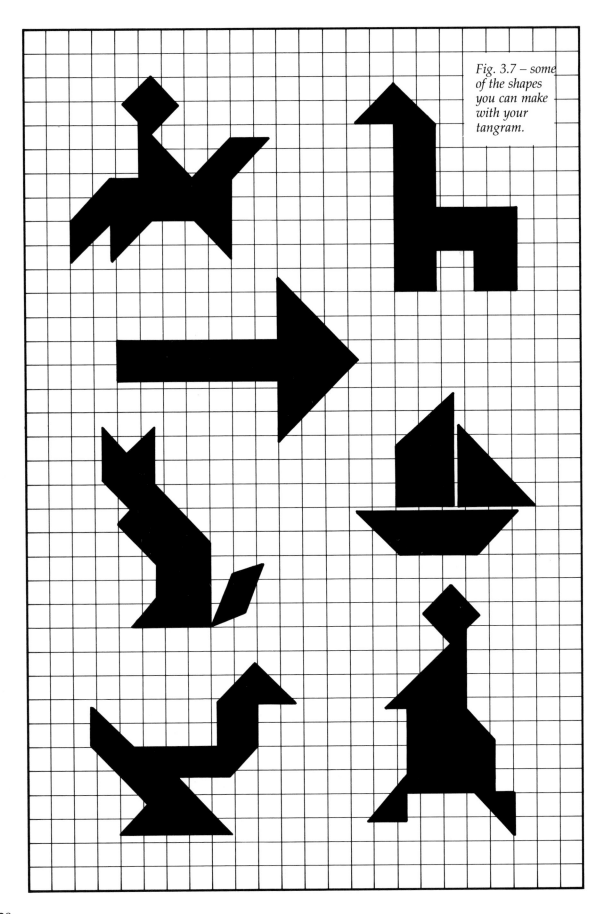

Fig. 3.7 – some
of the shapes
you can make
with your
tangram.

Elephant parade puzzle

About the puzzle

This puzzle is a beautifully complete plaything. The elephant-shaped puzzle pieces can be tipped out of their frame, stood up, and linked together trunk-to-tail – it is not for very small children, though.

At a scale of three grid squares to 25mm (1in), the puzzle measures 175mm (7in) wide and 238mm (9½ in) long (see fig. 4.1 on page 22). If you want the puzzle larger or smaller, just alter the scale to suit. The only tricky thing is the scroll-saw work, which does need to be precise. If you make a mess-up with one or other of the saw cuts, then it *will* show.

Making the puzzle

Drawing out the design and drilling

Draw the design up to full size and make a good clear tracing, using a soft pencil. Make sure that the plywood is free from splits, delaminations, stains, knots and tears. Use the pencil, compass, ruler and set-square to draw out on the wood the shape of the total outer frame. Ensure that the tracing is perfectly aligned by using tabs of masking tape to hinge the tracing to the top edge of the piece of 13mm (½ in) thick plywood.

Next, take a hard pencil and trace the lines through to the wood (fig. 4.2 – right). Then, with a 4mm (⅛ in)

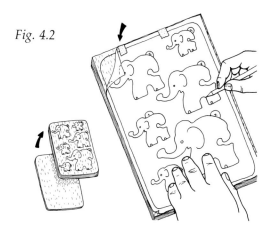

Fig. 4.2

Tools and materials

A sheet each of best-quality 13mm (½ in) thick and 4mm (⅛ in) thick white-faced multi-core plywood at 200 x 250mm (8 x 10in) (this allows for a small amount of cutting waste) • pencil • ruler • compass • set-square • an electric scroll-saw • two-tube resin wood-filler • a small hand drill with a 4mm (⅛ in) diameter drill bit • a small pin hammer • a few 6mm (¼ in) long brass pins/brads • white PVA wood glue • a pack of graded sandpapers • a good selection of toymakers' paints (acrylic – water-based – paint) in red, blue, yellow, green, orange, purple and black • clear high-gloss varnish • two paintbrushes – a broad-point and a fine-point.

diameter bit, drill pilot saw-blade holes through each of the little half-circle finger holes. Finally, pin the 4mm (⅛ in) thick sheet of ply – the backing board – to the underside of the 13mm (½ in) thick sheet.

Cutting out

Cut out the forms with the scroll saw. If you have to stop and start on a straight cut, the line will be stepped – so make sure you will not be interrupted.

It is also a good idea to make sure that the saw is fit for use! Give the scroll-saw cutting table a rub-over with wax polish, fit and tension a new fine-toothed saw blade, check that the cutting table is set at right angles to the blade, and generally see that the machine is in good working order. Start cutting out the straight-edged, curve-cornered frame.

Feed the work-piece into the moving blade, all the while making sure that the cut line is a fraction to the waste side of the drawn line, and that the moving blade is timely presented with the line of next cut. If you work at a nice gentle easy pace you will avoid tearing the wood, and the work-piece will leave the saw with the cut edge so perfectly smooth and shiny that it will not need rubbing down.

When you have cut out the total round-cornered frame shape, ease the two sheets of plywood apart, and put the thin backing sheet to one side (fig. 4.2 – left). Then take the top sheet back to the scroll saw,

Fig. 4.1 – working drawing and colour grid – the scale is three grid squares to 25mm (1in).

A group of standing and linking trunk-to-tail elephants set into a frame.

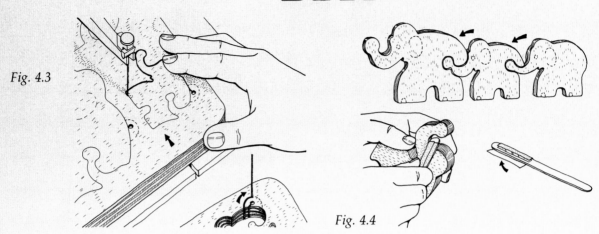

Fig. 4.3

Fig. 4.4

unhitch the top end of the saw blade, pass the blade through one or other of the drilled pilot holes, and refit and retension the blade (fig. 4.3 – top).

Next, switch on the power and very carefully cut out the smallest elephant profile. When you have cut it out, cut away the little half-circle that makes up the fingerhole (fig. 4.3 – bottom). Unhitch the blade and use the 'trunk' section of the smallest elephant cut-out to redraw and modify the link-up point of the next largest elephant (fig. 4.4 – top), and so you continue – from small to large – with all six cut-outs.

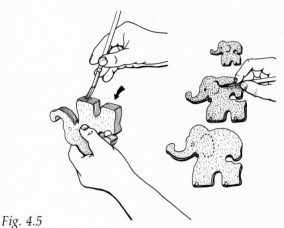

Fig. 4.5

Sanding, painting and varnishing

Next, sand the work down. Check the sawn edges for cavities, delaminations and tears – now is the time to make good with the two-tube resin filler (use as little as possible). Wait for the filler to dry and then sand all the sharp corners of the cut-outs, the holes and the frame edge down to a smooth, rounded-cornered finish (fig. 4.4 – bottom).

Then pin-fit the cut-frame on the back board and pencil-transfer the shape of the elephant cut-outs – the holes – through to the backing board.

When the work-piece is completely smooth-faced and round-cornered to the touch, ease the two boards apart, brush away the dust and debris, and paint them. Holding the cut-outs between thumb and index finger, lay the paint on in smooth thin coats. First paint the edges, then one side – of all six elephants – and then go back and paint the other sides (fig. 4.5 – left). There is no need to set up a drying frame or line – by the time all six elephants have been painted on the edge and side, the first elephant will be more less touch-dry. However, do stand the freshly painted animals on a clean surface such as scrap plywood or newspaper. When the acrylic paint is dry, use the fine brush and the black acrylic to pick out the little details – toes, ears and eyes – on both sides of the cut-outs (fig. 4.5 – right).

Next, paint the drawn shapes on the backing board, so that they match up with the colour of the cut-outs. So if the large elephant is yellow, then the large elephant on the backing board also needs to be yellow, and so on. When all the paint is dry, glue and pin-fix the two boards together and give the whole toy a few coats of clear varnish.

Finally, when the varnish is completely dry, give the edges of all the frame holes a wax polishing, so the animals are a smooth easy-slide push fit.

Useful advice

If you only have, say, 6mm (¼ in) thick plywood, then you could bond three sheets together to a total 18mm (¾ in) thickness.

When you are using the scroll saw, be careful not to go so slowly that you friction-burn the wood, nor so fast that the blade tears the face of the wood as it exits. If you have any doubts, have a try-out with a scrap of plywood.

It is most important that the cut edge be at right angles to the working face of the wood, so ensure that the scroll saw blade is well tensioned and the scroll saw cutting-table is correctly set so that it is at right angles to the lines of the saw blade.

Be careful when you are painting not to build up too much of a paint thickness on the edges of the elephants and the holes.

Cube puzzle

About the puzzle

Although the cube puzzle looks very simple, it is, in fact, quite a demanding project. It is swift to make, but for a successful result, great care and attention are needed. If all goes well, the cube puzzle can be shaped and cut in a couple of hours.

At a scale of four grid squares to 25mm (1in), the completed puzzle measures 38 x 38 x 38mm ($1^1/2$ x $1^1/2$ x $1^1/2$ in) (fig. 5.1). The puzzle is made up from a single cube of solid wood which is sawn into eight smaller, equally sized, interlocking cubes – this configuration is achieved by sawing the cube from two adjacent sides.

Each part of the cube should fit together well. Choosing a saw blade that is too thick will result in loosely fitting pieces. However, a saw blade that is too thin will produce pieces which fit too tightly once the appropriate finish is applied. So for the ideal fit, the right thickness of blade is essential – it is a good idea to practise first on a piece of waste wood.

The puzzle can be made to be more or less difficult to solve depending on how it is finished. To make the puzzle easier, you can avoid painting over the wood because the grain is an aid to assembling it correctly, or you could paint each part in colours that indicate the position of one piece in relation to another – when completed, each side of the cube

could be a different colour. I chose to paint each part of the cube a different colour, so after a while you can remember how the colours go together, but if you do not want to give away any clues, you can paint all the pieces the same colour all over.

Making the puzzle

Setting out the design

Ideally, the 38 x 38 x 38mm ($1^1/2$ x $1^1/2$ x $1^1/2$ in) cube should be cut from 38 x 38mm ($1^1/2$ x $1^1/2$ in) section stock that has every surface planed. If you cannot get this, however, you will need to prepare the wood yourself.

Take any oversize piece and plane two adjacent faces with the smoothing plane (with the work-piece held in the vice), making sure that they are at a right angle to each other. With the pencil and ruler, mark out 38mm ($1^1/2$ in) along the length of the rough side – measured from the edge of a planed side – and, using the scroll saw, cut to the waste side of this line. It only takes a few strokes of the plane to make the sawn surface smooth. Repeat this procedure on the second rough side – you then have a length of wood 38 x 38mm ($1^1/2$ x $1^1/2$ in) in section.

Measure and mark out a cube on the length of wood using the try-square. Again, saw to the waste side of the line. Smooth the opposite 'end grain' sides of the cube with grades of sandpaper.

Next, draw out the jigsaw design of both faces to full size and make an accurate tracing. Go over all lines with a soft pencil on the reverse side of the tracing, cut out the tracing of the two squares as one piece, and tape it in place on two adjacent faces of the cube (any face except an end-grain face).

When you are sure the tracing is correctly registered, take a hard pencil and transfer the design to the wood

---

Tools and materials

A piece of solid wood at 38 x 38 x 38mm ($1^1/2$ x $1^1/2$ x $1^1/2$ in), with all its sides planed smooth (jelutong cuts easily but you could use pine if that is easier to obtain) • a smoothing plane and a bench vice (only needed if you cannot get wood planed to size) • an electric scroll saw and a carefully selected blade • an A4 ($11^3/4$ x $8^1/4$ in) sheet of tracing paper • pencil • ruler • try-square • masking tape • a pack of graded sandpapers • sewing pins • modelling clay • a No. 6 paintbrush • acrylic paint in red, dark blue, yellow, purple, orange, green, light blue and pink • a small quantity of clear high-gloss varnish • white spirit.

Fig. 5.1 – working drawing: the scale is four grid squares to 25mm (1in).

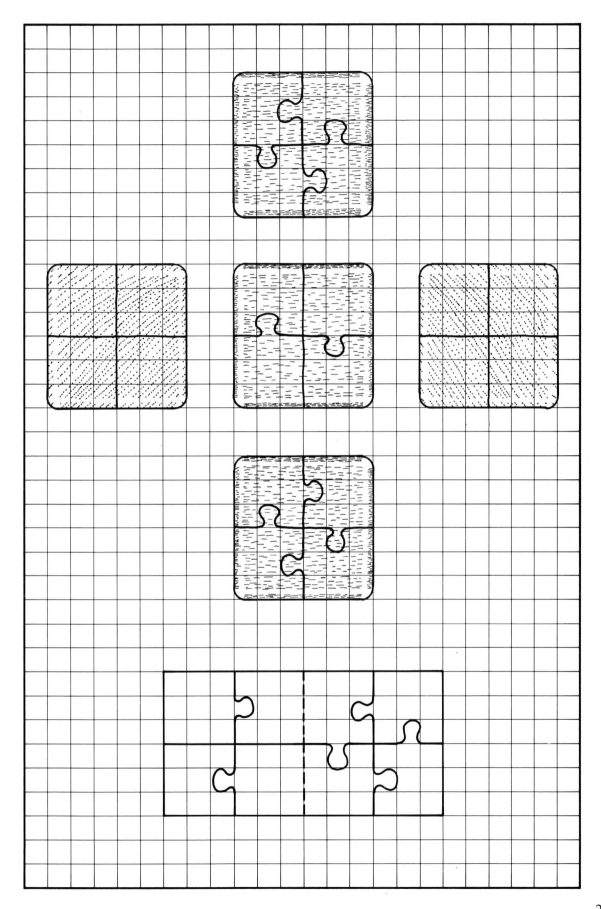

Fig. 5.2

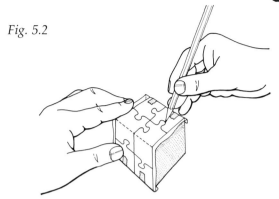

(fig. 5.2). Round off the cube's edges and corners with sandpaper, starting with the roughest and ending up with a fine paper. The cube should be beautifully smooth and comfortable to hold – no sharp corners and splinters! Before cutting, fill in 'by eye' any pencil lines which your sanding has obliterated.

Cutting out

Next, cut up the cube into its three-dimensional jigsaw parts. Begin with the side which has four 'tongue-and-mouth' parts uppermost. Make sure the saw blade is new and well tensioned and make the first cut across the cube so as to divide the cube in two (fig. 5.3 – top left). Wrap tape tightly around the cube along the line of the cut. You should just be able to make out the line of the next cut through the tape, but if you cannot, use the tracing to fill in the gap.

Fig. 5.3

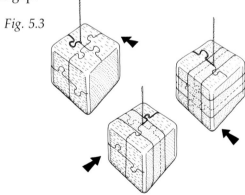

Make the second cut at a right angle to the first – this will divide the cube into four (fig. 5.3 – bottom). Again, wrap tape tightly around the cube along the line of this second cut. Turn the cube over and fill in the part of the line which has been obscured by tape. The last cut divides the cube into eight pieces (fig. 5.3 – right).

After removing all the tape, check that the 'tongues'

are sufficiently bulbous and necked so as not to slip out of the 'mouths'. Slide the puzzle apart and inspect the inside surfaces to see if they are correct.

Sanding, painting and varnishing

Now sand each of the eight parts to a good finish. There is no need to sand the ridges and troughs of the inside faces, but do soften any sharp edges and remove loose fibres (fig. 5.4 – left). Concentrate on resanding the outside faces to remove any damage to the surface caused by cutting and removal of the tape.

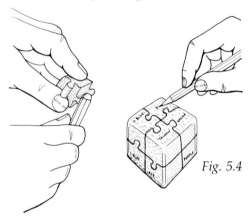

Fig. 5.4

Dilute some varnish with white spirit and seal all the pieces. When this is dry, sand the raised grain and rub off the nibs with fine sandpaper. Reassemble the puzzle and indicate with pencil the colour each piece is to be painted (fig. 5.4 – right).

Before you start painting, mount each piece on a pin – located in a trough so as to cause the least visible damage – and make a base for each pin from modelling clay (fig. 5.5 – left). Paint each part one face at a time, working from the centre outwards, using the pin to hold the piece. Draw the brush off the edges so as to avoid a build-up of paint on the adjacent side (fig. 5.5 – right).

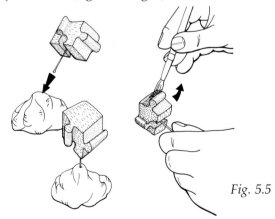

Fig. 5.5

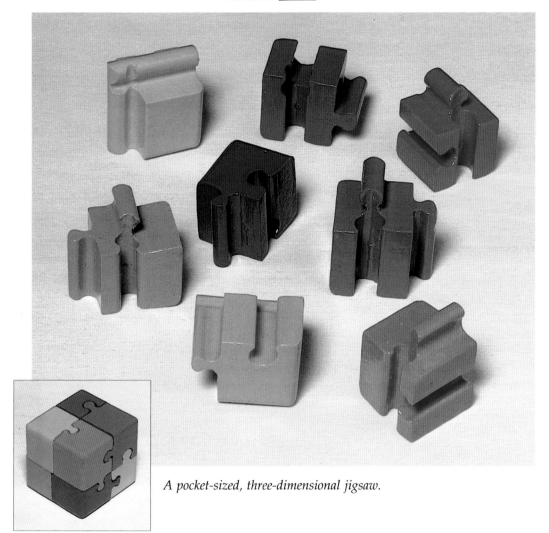

A pocket-sized, three-dimensional jigsaw.

Finally, when the paint is dry and you are satisfied with the coverage, give each piece a coat of gloss varnish. Allow a day for the varnish to dry, then reassemble the cube. If the pieces fit together too loosely, apply another coat of varnish, but if all is well the project is complete.

Useful advice

If you have trouble obtaining jelutong, when choosing an alternative remember that the wood needs to be soft so that it cuts nicely using a scroll saw but it also needs to be strong so that the projecting 'tongues' do not break off.

If you can more easily obtain wood that has been planed to a slightly different square section from the one I have specified, there is no reason not to use it. Adjust the scale of the jigsaw design accordingly using the grid as a guide.

When you have cut out the pieces, if you think a build-up of paint and varnish will make the puzzle fit together too tightly, stain and wax it instead.

Do not leave bits of the puzzle around where babies and small children are likely to find them – the brightly coloured, mouth-sized pieces are very attractive and could be mistaken for sweets.

Cats puzzle

About the puzzle

This jigsaw also has an interesting three-dimensional aspect: parts of it slot together to make five cat figures which stand up by themselves. The ginger fur-like look is created by blotching light and dark stain varnish over a white or yellow background, which is a traditional decorative technique called fossil stone marbling. This also camouflages the components of each cat among the many little jigsaw pieces. The front of the puzzle is marbled over a yellow background and the reverse side of the jigsaw pieces is marbled over a white background; the different paint effects make it a bit easier to fit the jigsaw pieces back into the frame.

The puzzle is made up from two rectangles of plywood. The top layer is painted with the fossil stone effect on both sides. It is then sandwiched between two waste layers and finally cut up into lots of small interlocking pieces surrounded by a frame, which is fixed on to the back or base layer.

At a scale of four grid squares to 25mm (1in), the puzzle measures 225m (9in) long and 150mm (6in) wide (fig. 6.1 on page 31). If you would like the puzzle bigger, adjust the scale. For example, a scale of three grid squares to 25mm (1in) would produce a puzzle 300mm (12in) long and 200mm (8in) wide.

Making this puzzle is a tricky business – any mistakes might ruin the whole project!

A traditional framed jigsaw that can be built into a family of five cats.

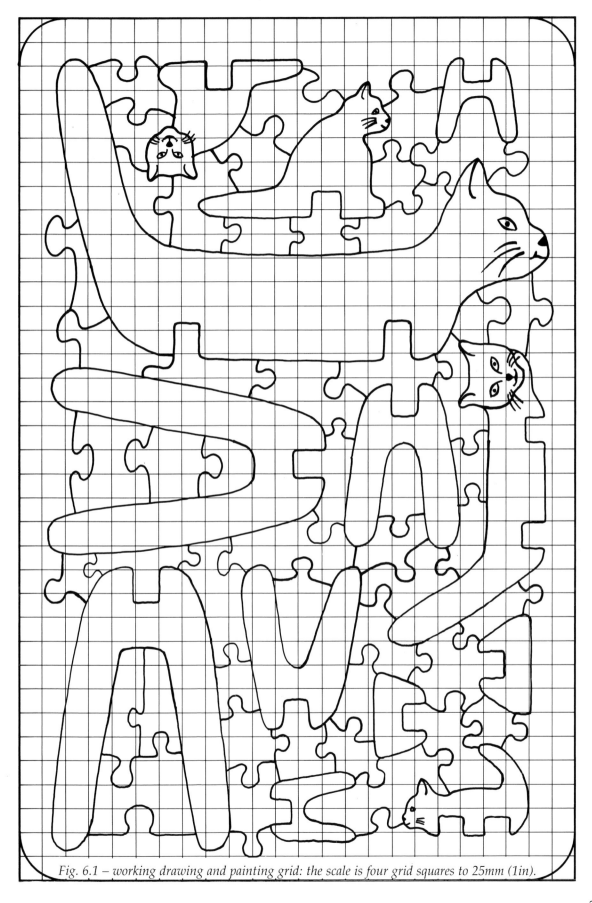

Fig. 6.1 – *working drawing and painting grid: the scale is four grid squares to 25mm (1in).*

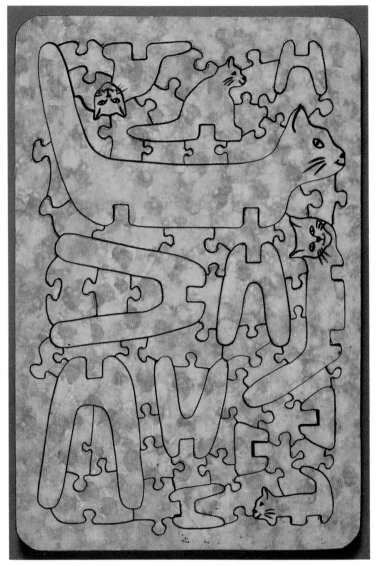

A traditional framed jigsaw that can be built into a family of five cats.

Making the puzzle

Marbling

From a good area of 6mm (¼ in) plywood, cut a rectangle 250 x 175mm (10 x 7in). Sand down both surfaces with sandpaper wrapped round a wooden block. Give one side a coat of yellow acrylic, let it dry, and then coat the other side with white. With your finest sandpaper, rub down the painted surfaces to remove any raised grain or nibs, then marble the white-painted side (the under-side of the jigsaw when the pieces are replaced in the frame).

Stir the stain varnish. Get two No. 6 brushes (one for each tin of varnish), a 13mm (½ in) decorator's brush, some clean cotton rags, and some white spirit. Cover about half the total area of white paint with generous, evenly distributed pea-size dabs of light oak varnish (see page 33: fig. 6.2 – top left).

As quickly as you can, fill in most of the remaining white area with similar dabs of Tudor oak varnish, reloading the brush after about every three dabs (fig. 6.2 – top right).

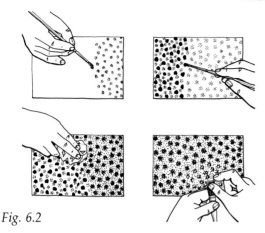

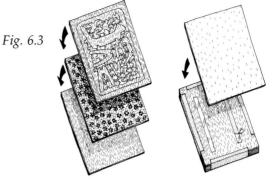

Fig. 6.3

Fig. 6.2

Then go over the whole area, dabbing the varnish with a screwed-up rag until the splotches of varnish begin to merge (fig. 6.2 – bottom left). Dip the 13mm (½ in) brush into the white spirit and speckle the whole area by flicking the bristles with a finger (fig. 6.2 – bottom right). White patches will appear in the varnish where the droplets of white spirit land. Then dab over the whole area again with the rag.

When the white marbled side is dry, repeat the whole procedure on the yellow side (the front of the jigsaw when the pieces are in the frame). Having already had the practice of painting one side, you can expect an even better result the second time around! Then paint both sides with one coat of varnish.

Drawing out the design

While waiting for the varnish to dry, cut out the remaining 250 x 175mm (10 x 7in) rectangle in best-quality 4mm (⅛ in) plywood, and the two waste pieces of the same dimensions (to protect both sides of the marbled layer while the puzzle is cut out).

Draw the design up to full size, and make a good tracing. Go over the reverse side of the tracing with a soft 2B pencil. Tape the tracing to one of the waste pieces, and press the design through to the wood with the HB pencil. Double-check that all the slots in the cat body parts are just fractionally wider than 4mm (⅛ in); the body parts need to slot together, so take into account the thickness of the plywood plus the thickness of the paint and varnish.

Next, place the waste pieces either side of the marbled jigsaw layer, yellow side up – the waste piece with the design drawn on it at the top – and tape the three layers together around the edges (fig. 6.3 – left). Stick the back to the under-side of this three-board sandwich, using double-sided tape (fig. 6.3 – right).

Cutting out

Hold the four-board sandwich so that part of it overhangs the edge of a sturdy work surface, and cut round the outside edge with the fretsaw. Rotate the work-piece as you progress and make sure the corners finish up evenly rounded (fig. 6.4 – left). Note the relative position of each layer by labelling the edges (not the waste layers), prise off the base layer, and then tape the three-board sandwich together again (fig. 6.4 – right).

Fig. 6.4

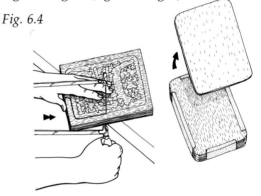

Choose any inconspicuous point on the jigsaw to drill the starting hole for the saw blade. Enter the blade through the hole, retension the saw, and start cutting as before. Cut all the way round one piece at a time until only the frame is left (fig. 6.5 – left).

Fig. 6.5

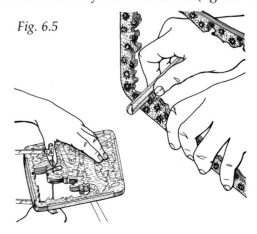

Do not cut out more than one piece at a time; once out of the frame, the waste layers will drop away, making it very difficult to finish cutting the pieces! The slots in the body parts *must* be the right width; when you come to cutting round the slots, be aware of the thickness of the saw blade and consider whether you need to cut to one side of your pencil line.

Separate the frame from the waste pieces by removing the tape from around the outside edges. Sort out the waste pieces and throw them away.

Assembling, staining and painting

Wrap some fine sandpaper around a lolly stick, or similar piece of wood, and rub down the inside edges of the frame and the outside edges of all the little jigsaw pieces to remove the loose fibres of wood and any roughness left by the saw (fig. 6.5 – right). Also sand down both faces of the base. Practise matching up the frame on the base (this is why you labelled the edges of each piece). When you are satisfied that everything will fit together nicely, roughen the underneath surface of the frame with sandpaper, then trail some superglue all round the under-side of the frame and position it on the base. Check immediately that the outside edges are flush, and then push down hard, so as to apply even pressure all over the surface (fig. 6.6.).

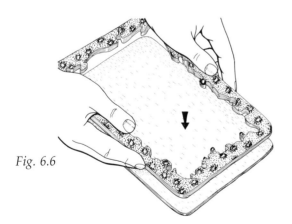

Fig. 6.6

If needed, sand the outside edges of the puzzle, then brush black ink over all the areas which are not already painted, including all the edges of the jigsaw pieces and the back of the puzzle. If you accidentally paint over the marbled surface, this is no problem; water-based ink wipes off with a damp cloth, even when dry.

Finally, draw in the faces of the cats, freehand or using your tracing, on both sides of the cut-outs. (The faces on the reverse side of the cats will be a mirror image of those on the front – you can reverse your tracing for this). Paint over the pencil lines with the No. 0 brush and black acrylic paint.

Now assemble the cats – three of them each slot on to two sets of legs, and the other two each slot into a base (fig. 6.7). Then you have the awesome task of replacing the jigsaw in the frame!

Fig. 6.7

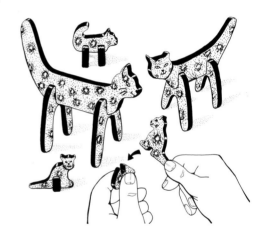

Useful advice

If the marbling goes wrong, wipe off as much varnish as you can with a large rag, pour white spirit over the surface, then wipe the surface clean and start again.

When cutting out the jigsaw pieces, with the waste wood either side, it is only too easy to make the mistake of cutting more than one piece out at a time. If this does happen, use your tracing to mark out the remaining cut lines directly on to the marbled surface. Use a V-board to complete the cutting, and take care not to damage the painted surface.

Panda puzzle

About the puzzle

This picture-scene puzzle with its seven pandas is quite easy to make. The puzzle is made up from two layers of plywood (see fig. 7.1 on page 36); a thin piece forms the base or back board, and the frame and jigsaw are cut together from a single sheet of thicker plywood. Only the frame is fixed to the face: this is a cutting project, with very little construction involved.

With the working drawing at a scale of four grid squares to 25mm (1in), the puzzle measures 222mm (8⁷/₈in) long and 150mm (6in) wide. The puzzle might be awkward if it were smaller, but if you want it bigger, just scale up the design.

Making the puzzle

Drawing out the design

Draw the design on paper (full size), or get an enlarged photocopy. Trace the design in all its detail and, using the 2B pencil, go over all the lines on the reverse side.

Avoid irregular wood and choose the flattest, smoothest and whitest areas for the best results. Using the cross-cut saw, cut two rectangles approximately 250mm (10in) long and 175mm (7in) wide (this allows an area of wastage of roughly

13mm (¹/₂in) around the puzzle): one from 6mm (¹/₄in) thick ply and the other from 4mm (¹/₈in) thick ply. Stick the two rectangles together temporarily using strips of double-sided tape (fig. 7.2 – left).

Fig. 7.2

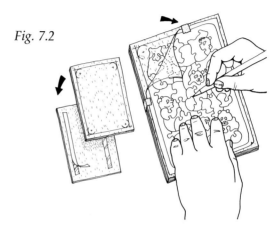

With the thicker layer facing upwards, mark out the perimeter of the puzzle using the pencil, ruler, set-square and compasses. Align the tracing with the pencil outline, fix it down with masking tape, and go over the lines with the HB pencil. The soft pencil on the reverse of the tracing will be transferred to the wood (fig. 7.2 – right).

At this stage, do not mark out the features of the faces which are painted on later rather than cut out, or things could get confusing!

Cutting out

A fretsaw and a piercing saw are used for this project because only a few fine blades can handle the jigsaw arrangement. While you could use a fretsaw for the entire project, a piercing saw is more suitable for the smaller pieces.

Begin by cutting through both layers of plywood along the outline of the rectangle, using the fretsaw (fig. 7.3 – top). It is difficult to achieve a cut which is perfectly square with both faces when sawing through this thickness of material, but as this forms the outside edge, squareness is not so important.

Tools and materials

A sheet each of best-quality white-faced plywood 6mm (¹/₄in) thick and 4mm (¹/₈in) measuring 250 x 175mm (10 x 7in) (this takes into account a small amount of cutting waste) • HB and 2B pencils • ruler • set-square • compass • A4 (11³/₄ x 8¹/₄ in) tracing paper • a fretsaw and fine blade • a piercing saw and V-board • a large flat-bladed cross-cut saw • a small hand drill with a 1.5mm (¹/₁₆in) diameter drill bit • a lightweight pin hammer • about six 6mm (¹/₄in) brass or steel pins • white PVA wood glue • double-sided tape • a pack of graded sandpapers • acrylic paint (or an equivalent) in black, white, dark green, light green and mid green • clear gloss varnish • a 13mm (¹/₂in) decorator's brush • No. 1 and No. 6 artist's paintbrushes.

*Fig. 7.1 –
working
drawing and
colour
diagram: the
scale is four
grid squares
to 25mm
(1in).*

*A
traditional
framed
jigsaw
picture
featuring
seven
individual
pandas.*

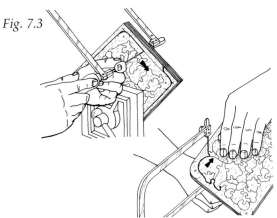

Fig. 7.3

– right). In some places it does not matter if you stray from the line as long as you maintain a smooth curve and do not lose the 'character' of the pandas.

Sanding, painting and varnishing

Next, remove any roughness and loose wood fibres with sandpaper. Pay most attention to the underside of the puzzle, which suffers from splintering (fig. 7.5 – top).

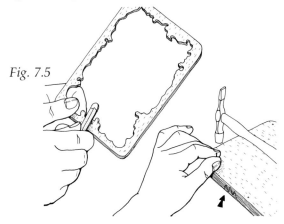

Fig. 7.5

However, the cut should run smoothly around the corners of the rectangle.

Scribble a 'registration' mark on one side of the rectangle sandwich so you can match the two pieces later on, then prise the boards apart. Remove the double-sided sticky tape, put aside the thinner board, and take up the thicker one with all the cutting lines marked. With the 1.5mm ($^{1}/_{16}$ in) diameter drill bit, or perhaps a small steel nail used as a bit, drill all the way through at any point along the line indicating the inside edge of the frame.

Enter the blade of the fretsaw through this hole, retension the saw, and cut all the way round in order to separate the frame from the central section (fig. 7.3 – bottom). Unhitch the saw and put the frame aside. The central section is cut up in a similar way to a jigsaw. First, cut out each panda as a complete shape with the fretsaw – a continuous cut gives the pandas their smooth outline (fig. 7.4 – top).

Then, using the piercing saw and a V-board, cut up each panda into its parts, remembering that each part must interlock with the next (fig. 7.4 – left). Finish up by reducing the parts surrounding the pandas (fig. 7.4

Take the frame and the back board and practise matching up the pencil registration marks. Spread a thin film of PVA glue over the reverse side of the frame and put the pieces back together, checking that the edge is flush on all sides. With the back board facing up on the bench, tap in the six pins – these hold the work-piece together while it is glued and add strength (fig. 7.5 – bottom). Wipe any excess glue off with a damp cloth. Prior to painting, seal everything with diluted varnish, using a 13mm ($^{1}/_{2}$ in) brush for the frame and back board and a No. 6 brush for the little pieces. When dry, remove all the roughness or 'nibs' with the finest sandpaper.

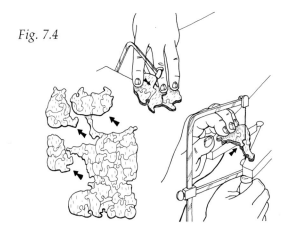

Fig. 7.4

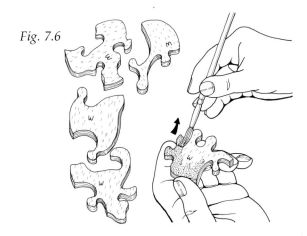

Fig. 7.6

Replace all the parts within the frame and indicate the colour of each piece with pencil, using the colour diagram as reference – do not press too hard. Remove all the pieces again, and paint them (fig. 7.6 – left). (Only the top surfaces of the frame and the loose pieces are painted). Using the No. 6 brush, start from the centre of each piece and work outwards off the edges (fig. 7.6 – right).

Once dry, you might find that only the white areas need a second coat. Again, replace all the parts in the frame, and use your original tracing to mark out the features of the pandas (fig. 7.7 – left). Use black acrylic and a No. 1 brush to fill in these details, or a fine-pointed permanent black pen (fig. 7.7 – right).

Finally, with all the pieces out of the frame, give all surfaces (except the edges of each piece) two coats of clear gloss varnish. By now, no doubt, you are quite fed up with doing the puzzle!

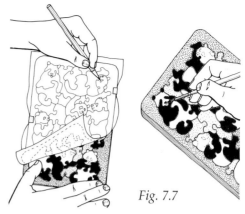

Fig. 7.7

Useful advice

As so few 6mm (¹/₄ in) pins are needed, if you do not have any, just reduce longer pins to the right length by snipping off the heads with a pair of pliers.

Victorian gymnasts puzzle

About the puzzle

With the working drawing at a scale of four grid squares to 25mm (1in), the puzzle measures 213mm (8¹/₂ in) long and 150mm (6in) wide (see fig. 8.1 on page 40). You will see that the puzzle is made from three layers: a sliding lid, the gymnasts, and the back or base (figs. 8.2 and 8.3 on page 41). The lid and the frame within which the lid slides are made from one piece of wood. The scroll-saw table is set so that the blade cuts at a 45° angle through the thickness of the work-piece.

When the frame part is fixed down, the lid is also held down but can slide in and out within the frame. The sliding lid is really easy to make.

In the centre layer, all the figures are cut out from one sheet of plywood. The remaining frame and the pieces that fit around the figures are stuck to the base, giving the impression of a maze. So this puzzle is different from the ordinary frame puzzle and is harder to make. However, I am sure you will have no problems!

The shape of each gymnast figure relates to the same square module – meaning that a figure takes up either a whole or a half square. In either case,

Tools and materials

A sheet of best-quality 13mm (¹/₂ in) thick white-faced multi-core plywood at 238 x 175mm (9¹/₂ x 7in) and two sheets of the same dimensions in 4mm (¹/₈ in) (this allows for a small amount of cutting waste) • double-sided tape • A4 (11³/₄ x 8¹/₄ in) tracing paper • A4 (11³/₄ x 8¹/₄ in) card • HB and 2B pencils • ruler • compass • set-square • an electric scroll saw with an adjustable angle table • a small hand drill with a 1.5mm (¹/₁₆ in) diameter drill bit • a 13mm (¹/₂ in) chisel • a shallow gouge just under 13mm (¹/₂ in) across (or a penknife) • mallet • small pin hammer • forty 13mm (¹/₂ in) brass pins • PVA wood glue • a 13mm (¹/₂ in) decorator's brush • three No. 1 brushes and one No. 0 • a pack of graded sandpapers • clear cellulose paints in red, light blue and yellow • cellulose thinner • black acrylic paint • light oak stain varnish.

heads, backs, hands and feet form the outline of the allotted whole or half square space. The figures are designed to be stacked together in any way you choose.

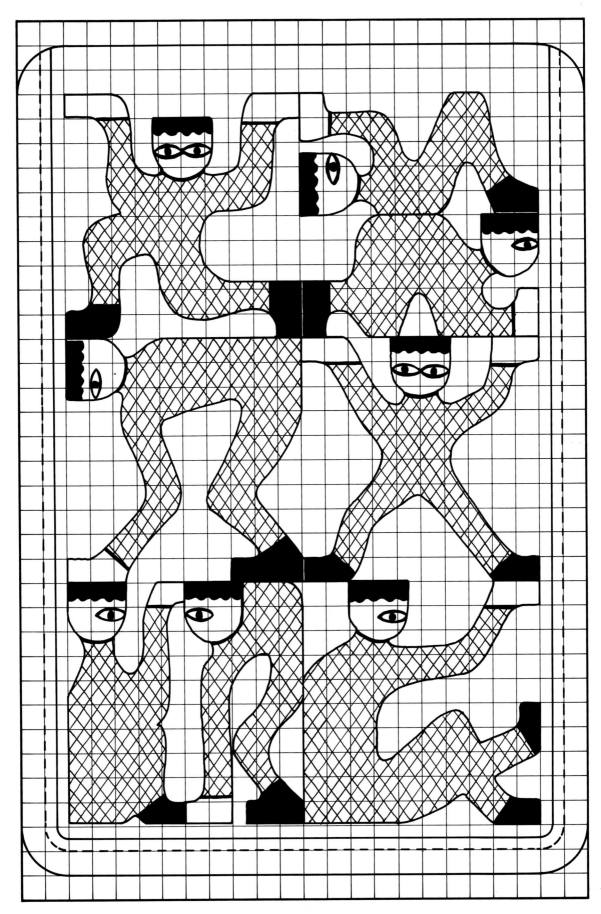

Making the puzzle

Drawing out the design

Redraw the design to full size using the scale grid as a guide. Use a ruler to draw the parts of the figures which form the outline of the square or half square, then make a tracing of it and go over every line with a 2B pencil on the reverse side.

Select the plywood in the two thicknesses needed. Mark out rough rectangles at 238 x 175mm (9½ x 7in) – avoid places that have been filled and other faulted areas like cavities, stains, or torn grain – and then cut them out with a scroll saw. Sand down any ripped grain left by the saw. Stick the plywood together with double-sided tape to make a three-board sandwich with the two 4mm (⅛ in) pieces either side of the 13mm (½ in) thickness.

Choose the best side of the plywood sandwich, label it 'top' in pencil, then construct the outline of the puzzle with a ruler, set-square and compass. Cut along your pencil line with the scroll saw to remove the waste, making the corner curves as even as possible. Make a registration mark on the edge of the sandwich (for matching up later) and then prise the layer apart, removing the tape in the process.

Tape your tracing to the top piece and transfer the

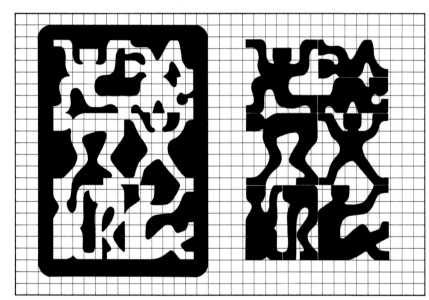

Fig. 8.2 – design templates for the centre layer pieces and the figures: the scale is five grid squares to 50mm (2in).

Fig. 8.3 – design templates for the lid pieces and the base: the scale is five grid squares to 50mm (2in).

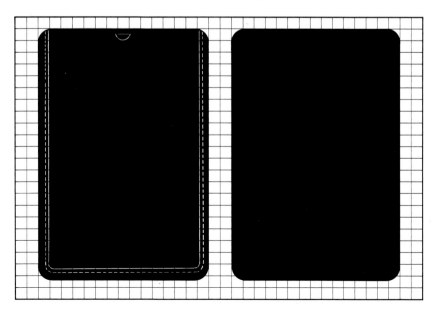

Fig. 8.1 – working drawing and colour grid: the scale is four grid squares to 25mm (1in).

details of the lid only – going over the tracing again with an HB pencil will print the soft pencil lines on to the wood from the reverse side of the tracing.

Remove the tracing – check that all the details are clear – and reposition it on the 13mm (½ in) piece. Transfer the outlines of all the figures, but do not bother with the faces, hands, or feet.

Cutting out

Cut out the lid first. Set the saw table at 45° and practise following a straight line – you might find cutting a bevel is more difficult than normal operations. Rehearse feeding the work-piece into the blade.

Now start at the top left-hand corner of the puzzle so that the work-piece is rotated clockwise as the cutting continues at each corner (fig. 8.4 – left).

Fig. 8.4

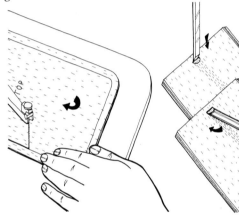

Check that the lid slides nicely in the frame. Any wobbles in the saw cut will interfere with a good fit, so smooth out bumps with sandpaper wrapped round a block of wood.

For carving out the fingertip recess in the sliding lid, use a 13mm (½ in) chisel for chopping in the initial straight cut and then a gouge for scooping out the recess (fig. 8.4 – right). If you use a penknife, start by making several straight cuts – scoring deeper each time – and then carve out the recess by taking a number of shavings, digging deeper each time. Be careful not to take away too much wood and make a hole through the lid!

Take up the middle section with the figures already marked out, and select a point at which to drill the starting hole for the saw blade. The 1.5mm (¹⁄₁₆ in) hole is best placed at a junction rather than somewhere along a line. Choose a thin blade to pass through the hole, and keep it well tensioned. There

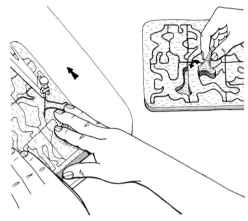

Fig. 8.5

is no need to cut the figures out in any particular order, but be sure not to lose *any* plywood pieces – all the little bits are used (fig. 8.5 – left).

Before going any further, give all parts of the puzzle a preliminary sanding, mainly to remove any loose figures and irregularities.

Assembling

Take the back piece and the frame surround of the 13mm (½ in) centre layer and practise putting the two together using the scribbled registration mark as a guide. Put the centre frame face down on a bench top, spread a thin film of PVA glue on the reverse side, and put the back layer in position. Use six 13mm (½ in) brass pins – equally spaced around the very edge of the puzzle – to fix the back to the frame. Any excess glue can be wiped off with a clean damp rag.

Turn the work-piece the right way up and replace all the figures and the surrounding 'islands' of wood. Then take out each 'island' of wood, one at a time, spread a thin film of PVA glue on the underside of it, and replace it (fig. 8.5 – right).

When you have applied glue to every loose piece that is not a figure, hold a piece of stiff card over the top surface, flip the puzzle over and lay it back on the bench. Use the tracing (wrong side up) to mark the positions of pins on the back of the puzzle, so that they coincide with the 'islands' beneath (fig. 8.6 – left). Use no fewer than two pins to fix each piece, no matter how small.

As before, use the registration mark to locate the frame for the sliding lid on the puzzle layer.

A traditional boxed set of gymnast figures that can be built into an infinite variety of configurations.

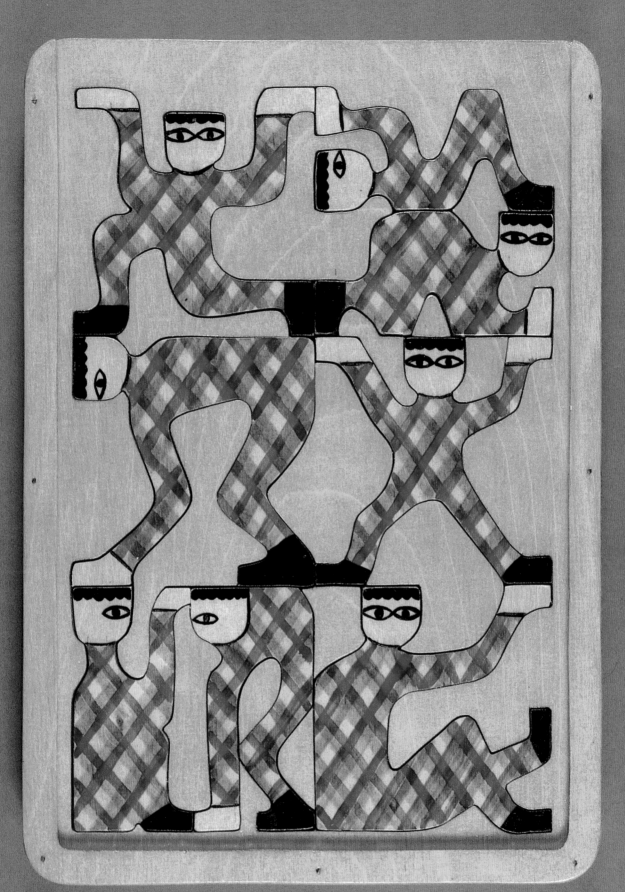

For the lid to slide in and out nicely, the frame needs to be positioned in exactly the right place. Use PVA glue and seven equally spaced brass pins; the outside edges of the puzzle should be completely flush. Check that the lid works nicely by sliding it in and out of the frame a few times.

Painting and varnishing

Remove all the figures from the box and seal them with diluted varnish. Use the finest sandpaper to smooth down raised grain and remove nibs. Use the tracing to fill in the face, hands and feet details of each gymnast and to indicate the direction of the overlaid clear-colour pattern.

Stick masking tape over the faces and hands which are to be left as natural wood, and cut the tape – using a sharp knife – to fit the shapes, and score the surface of the wood at the same time. This stops the paint bleeding over a line.

Take one No. 1 brush for each of the three colours. Paint a line of red in one direction, right across a figure, and next to this, with no gap, a line of blue, then a line of yellow. Continue painting lines in that order until the whole surface is covered. The paint dries fast, but watch out for colours running into one another.

Work across each figure in this way, and when this first application is dry, repeat the procedure, but this time paint the lines at an angle of just off 90° to the first lines (fig. 8.6 – right). You will get a

Fig. 8.6

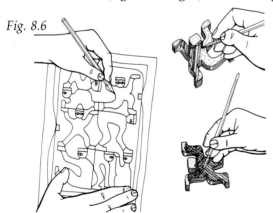

regular pattern of diamonds in red, blue and yellow, and also purple, green and orange. Finally, fill in the black details – eyes, hair, collars, cuffs and shoes – using black acrylic paint and a No. 0 brush, painting all the figures on both sides.

Apply a coat of clear gloss varnish to both sides of each figure, avoiding the edges. Treat the box, including the lid, with light-oak stain varnish. Sand the box down after the first coat to remove any

roughness, and then apply a further two coats to build up a rich brown lustre.

Useful advice

If you ruin one part of the puzzle, instead of starting all over again or giving up, make another part. For example, if you damage one of the figures by cutting into it by accident, just finish cutting the shape out and then use it as a template. Make sure the grain of the replacement runs in the same direction, and when sawing, ensure that the pencil line is wasted. In this way, the figure will fit snugly in place and no one will be able to tell the difference!

If you have difficulty in hammering the pins in straight without their bending, use long-nosed pliers rather than your finger and thumb to hold the pins.

When the box is varnished, if the lid is too tight a fit and jams, try lightly sanding the bevelled edge of the lid and applying candle wax to it.

Two gymnasts practising their acrobatics.

An A-Z of primary puzzle-making tools, materials and techniques

Acrylic paint – A water-based paint that can be used straight from the can/tube, and is ideal for woodworking projects. It is quick-drying, so you can recoat colours without delay – though it usually only takes one coat to cover – and comes in a huge variety of colours. The brushes are easy to wash in water. Once dry, acrylics are durable and completely non-toxic, but please protect the painted surfaces with one or two coats of clear high-gloss varnish.

Auger drill bit – A drill bit which is usually used for drilling larger diameter holes than the normal twist bit. Auger bits produce good clean holes, but they can only be used in conjunction with a hand drill brace, and they are slow work.

Bevelling – A process which creates a sloping edge or surface. Use an electric scroll saw, with the table tilted.

Bird's mouth cutting board – A board with a 'V' shape cut out of it, which can be clamped to a surface or held in a vice. It is normally used when cutting out very small flat wood pieces, in conjunction with either a piercing saw or a fretsaw. The board supports the work-piece and allows the saw to be manoeuvred within the 'V'. Also called a V-board.

Brace – A hand-operated drill, normally used with an auger bit or hole saw to drill large-diameter holes.

Brushes – We use two types. Decorator's brushes are good for large areas, and are described by their width. For example, a 13mm (½ in) brush might be good for varnishing the back of a puzzle. Artist's watercolour brushes are described by a number series which is written on the shaft. A No. 0 is very fine and is used to paint very fine lines, and a No. 6 is suitable for filling in quite large areas. The brushes must be washed out really well each time they are used, and before the paint, varnish or whatever has had time to dry, otherwise they may be useless for the next project. For washing out acrylic paint, PVA glue, and water-based inks, and anything else that is water-based, use water. For varnish and stain varnish, and anything else oil-based, use white spirit and then washing-up liquid to clean the brush. For cellulose

paint, and any other cellulose products, clean your brushes with cellulose thinner.

Cellulose clear paint – A quick-drying transparent paint that is especially good for overlaying to give good colour-mixing effects. It also shows off the wood grain beneath.

Cellulose thinner – A solvent for cellulose paint. It can be used for diluting thick paint, and is essential for cleaning brushes.

Chisels – Chisels are designed for chopping out wood and are used in conjunction with a mallet. A chisel should be used without a mallet when the wood is soft enough to cut easily, or if the chisel is delicate. Chisels are good for cutting up to a line, and are described according to their width.

Clamps (cramps) – Clamps are useful for puzzle-making, but not always necessary. Both G-clamps and holdfast clamps are good for clamping wood to a surface while it is being worked. Always protect the work-piece by having some waste wood between it and the jaws/head of the holdfast/clamp. Instead of clamps, you could use a heavy weight, or you can screw a bridge of wood over the work-piece, or you can get somebody to help you.

Coping saw – A versatile saw used for cutting complicated profiles or holes in thin-section wood. It has the unique advantage of a pivoting blade; swivelling spigots at both ends of the frame allow the blade to cut in any direction. Rather than rotating the work-piece around the blade, you manoeuvre the coping saw around the work-piece, so it can handle pieces that are almost twice as wide as the frame is deep – and the blades are really easy to fit.

Cross-cut saw – A large general-purpose saw which has a very deep whippy, flexible blade, used for cutting straight lines only. One about 600mm (24in) long, with 8–9 teeth every 25mm (1in) (i.e. a pitch of 3mm), is most suitable for cutting out rough rectangles from large sheets of plywood.

Double-sided tape – Like adhesive tape, but sticky on both sides, it is ideal for holding pieces of plywood together in a sandwich while cutting out identical multiple shapes.

Dowel – Round-section wood that is sold in a variety of diameters. In puzzle-making, sandpaper wrapped around a dowel makes an excellent tool for sanding the edges of jigsaw pieces.

Drilling holes – Various drills and drill bits are used for boring different holes. The size of a hole is measured by its diameter and, where appropriate, its depth. A hand twist drill and twist bits are used to drill small-diameter holes. A small hole is needed for fitting a screw and also for passing a saw blade through. For larger-diameter holes, use either a hand-held electric drill with a flatbit or a hole saw, or a drill brace with an auger bit or hole saw. If you want a 'clean' hole, before you start drilling, clamp the work-piece to a surface with a waste scrap of wood sandwiched beneath.

Electric drill – A high-speed hand-held drill which can be used to bore any size hole with twist bits, flatbits or hole saws.

Finishing – The last stages in making: sanding with graded sandpapers, filling (if necessary), staining and painting, varnishing or waxing.

Flatbit – A drill bit, usually for boring large-diameter holes. It must be operated at high speed, so can only be used with an electric drill. It is the cheapest of all large-diameter drill bits, fine for most jobs, and the simplest to resharpen.

Fretsaw – Designed for cutting out complicated profiles and holes in sheet material, the fretsaw (illustrated in fig. 1.5 on page 8) can handle quite large pieces of wood. The blade does not pivot so the work-piece must be manoeuvred around the blade. A variety of blades are available, the teeth of which always face downwards so the saw cuts on the downstroke. The fretsaw is normally used with a bird's mouth cutting board or V-board.

Gouge – A wood-carving tool with a spoon-shaped end which is used for scooping out hollows.

Hardboard – A very cheap manufactured wood board, normally 4mm ($\frac{1}{8}$ in) thick, which can be used as protective waste pieces in puzzle-making.

Hole saw – A combination of a drill bit and a cylindrical saw blade, used for cutting out large-diameter holes. A hole saw can be used in a drill brace, but it is quicker to use an electric drill.

Inks – Colours which soak into the surface of porous materials. In this book, water-based inks are using for staining wood.

Jelutong – An excellent timber for making solid wood block puzzles. It is soft enough to cut easily with lightweight saws, and is surprisingly strong for its density.

Laminating – This involves gluing together two or more layers of sheet material. Many of the puzzles are constructed in this manner.

Mallet – A handle with a large block of wood at the end: the equivalent of a hammer. It is used to drive chisels through wood.

Marbling – A surface treatment which gives the impression of marble. It is a traditional technique which can be achieved by a number of ways. One method involves blending two different colours of stain varnish over a light-coloured background.

Masking tape – A self-adhesive, low-tack paper tape used for masking, for fixing tracings on to wood, or for holding pieces of wood together while they are sawn.

Modelling clay – A soft, 'plastic' mouldable material which holds a shape without ever hardening. It can be shaped around sewing pins, and used to support small puzzle pieces whilst they are being painted or varnished.

Nibs – An informal term which serves to describe the tiny raised fibres which appear on the surface of wood after it has been sealed.

Painting – This involves covering areas of wood with acrylic or cellulose paint, and for this a variety of brushes are used. Large areas of colours should be painted as evenly as possible, which requires a methodical approach. Small painted details require a steady hand and a great deal of care. Find a spotlessly clean and dust-free area to paint in. While drying, the puzzle pieces may need to be supported; possibly hanging from a line, or supported by sewing pins with modelling-clay bases.

Painting grids – For each project, different colours have been chosen for each area. These areas are indicated on a scaled grid.

Pencils – HB pencils are used for most things, but a soft 2B pencil is good for going over a drawing on the reverse side of a tracing before the design is transferred to the wood.

Penknife – A small pocket knife with a blade that folds into the handle. If the blade has a slender rounded end, and is sharp, then it is a useful carving tool. When working with a penknife, always cut away from your other hand, and beware of the blade folding on to your fingers.

Piercing saw – A piercing saw is excellent for cutting out tiny jigsaw pieces. It can be used with a V-board or bird's mouth cutting board, and relatively coarse blades are best for cutting plywood. The blade does not pivot, so the work-piece has to be rotated around the blade. Blades break easily, but the larger part of a broken blade can be refitted in the adjustable frame.

Pine – The cheapest, most easily obtainable wood which is soft to work. It can be bought in standard sections which are planed smooth on all surfaces. Pine does split easily, though, which makes it less suitable for puzzles than jelutong.

Pin hammer – A small lightweight hammer specially designed for knocking in pins.

Pins – Small nails which are knocked into wood and are hardly noticeable afterwards. Brass pins look nicer than steel pins, but steel pins are less expensive. In puzzle-making, pins are used to fix one layer of wood to another while glue dries. As pins are so small, it is easier to hold them with long-nosed pliers while you hammer them in.

Plane – A hand-held tool used for smoothing and levelling wood. The removable blade needs to be kept very sharp for the plane to work nicely. Once you have got the hang of using the tool, it will become invaluable.

Pliers – Primarily a gripping tool, pliers can normally be used for cutting as well. They come in many shapes and sizes, but we use long-nosed pliers, which are excellent for holding tiny pins and good for cutting pins shorter.

Plywood (multi-core plywood or multi-ply) – Plywood is a manufactured board made from multiple thin sheets of wood which are glued together with the grain in half the layers running at 90° to the grain in the other layers. The advantage of this construction is that slender projecting parts – like the delicate pieces in a jigsaw – do not snap off, which would be likely in solid wood. We always use best-quality birch/white-faced plywood because it cuts without splintering. Birch plywood

can be obtained in thicknesses from 4mm ($^1/_8$in) to 25mm (1in) and is sold in sheets 1200 x 2400mm (48 x 96in). You may be able to buy bargain off-cuts, but it is usually more economical to buy a whole sheet, rather than small pieces. However, if you do not wish to buy lots of different thicknesses, it is perfectly reasonable to buy just one 4mm ($^1/_8$in) thick sheet, and then laminate pieces to make up the other thicknesses you require. Plywood can be cut with a cross-cut saw, a fretsaw, a coping saw, a piercing saw or an electric scroll saw. Edges can be planed, and both edges and faces can be sanded.

PVA glue (polyvinyl acetate) – A white, ready-to-use, water-based wood glue that dries clear. Glued surfaces must be held together firmly while the PVA dries: use clamps, pins or masking tape. It takes a few minutes before it starts to dry, so there is some time for making adjustments. It is good for laminating layers of plywood and, diluted, it can be used for gluing and stretching paper on to wood.

Rags – Scraps of clean cloth – cotton sheet is best – which are good for cleaning off excess glue, applying and polishing a wax finish, or for blending colours during the marbling process.

Registration mark – This is a scribbled pencil mark drawn on the edges of two or more layers of plywood which share the same outline. After separating the boards, there can be no mistake in repositioning them the right way, as long as the scribbled line is registered correctly.

Sanding and sandpaper – Sandpaper, also called glass paper or garnet paper, is used for removing loose fibres of wood after sawing, rounding off sharp corners, making edges and surfaces smooth, and removing nibs after sealing wood. These operations are generally referred to as sanding or rubbing down. Different grades of sandpaper, from rough to smooth, are needed for puzzle-making, and are available separately or as a mixed pack. When sanding a large flat surface, use two or three grades and finish up with the finest; wrap the sandwich around a block of wood, press hard against the work-piece, and rub up and down in the direction of the grain. When you are sanding long straight edges, continue to use a block, but for complicated jigsaw profiles, wrap the sandwich around a dowel, lolly stick or similar stick of wood. The very finest sandpaper is best for removing the nibs from a sealed surface; scuff lightly across the wood with a scrap of sandpaper in your hand.

Sandwiching – In this book, sandwiching refers to stacking layers of plywood together and cutting through the stack to produce a number of identical pieces. Double-sided tape is used as a temporary fixing between layers. A piece of plywood can also be sandwiched between two pieces of waste wood, fixed together with masking tape, to protect the centre layer while it is cut.

Scroll saw – An electric table saw, which does the same job as a fretsaw but cuts faster and more accurately – for cutting out profiles or holes in thin sheets of wood. The work-piece is manoeuvred around the blade in the same way as a fretsaw. The scroll saw is safe to use, but the blade jigs up and down very fast, so hold the work-piece firmly down on the surface.

Sealing – Wood is usually sealed to make a good surface before paint or varnish is applied. One coat of diluted varnish is ideal. Once the varnish is dry, the surface can be sanded to remove the nibs and then the finish can be applied.

Set-square – A drawing instrument used for establishing right angles.

Sewing pin – A short steel pin with a rounded broadened head and a sharp point. They can be stuck into modelling-clay bases and used to support small pieces of puzzle while they are being painted or varnished.

Staining – A thin wash of grain-enhancing colour which soaks into the surface without building up a thickness. Water-based inks can be used.

Stain varnish – A coloured varnish which is usually applied to light-coloured woods to make them look like a darker variety.

Superglue – A very strong, exceptionally fast-drying glue which sticks most materials. No clamping is required, but the positioning has to be right first time as there are no second chances. Superglue can stick your fingers together, so do take care!

Tape clamping – A way of holding pieces of wood together with strips of masking tape. Tape clamping can be useful when a project involves making several cuts – at different angles – all the way through the same piece of wood.

Tracing paper – Used for transferring the lines of a design from a full-size drawing to the wood. When you trace off a design, or transfer a design to the wood, always make sure that the tracing paper is well secured with tabs of masking tape.

Try-square – A woodworking tool, used for marking lines at 90° from a straight edge.

Twist bit – A drill bit used for boring small-diameter holes. It can be used in a twist drill or an electric drill.

Twist drill – A small hand-held drill designed for boring small-diameter holes with twist bits.

Varnish – We use clear gloss polyurethane varnish to finish natural bare wood or to protect surfaces that are painted with acrylic colours.

V-board – See bird'smouth cutting board.

Vice – A bench-mounted clamping device that is used for holding and securing wood while it is being worked.

Waxing – An alternative finish to varnish which can be applied over a natural bare wood surface or stained wood. Furniture wax is spread on with a clean cotton rag and buffed up once the wax sets. Reapply the wax whenever the surface goes dull.

White spirit – A colourless solvent for most oil-based products. It can be used for diluting varnish or washing brushes which have been used for varnishing.

Workbench – A workbench is a specifically designed table for carrying out woodworking operations. However, you could use a sturdy kitchen table.

Working drawing – A drawing which describes the dimensions and construction of a puzzle. In this book, every project appears on a scaled grid. If, for example, the scale of the grid is described in the text as being four grid squares to 25mm (1in) on the full-scale article, when you make a full-size drawing, just draw up a full-size grid and transfer the image one square at a time. If you prefer, you can speed up the process by using a photocopier: simply enlarge the grid squares up to the scale size.

Work-piece – Part or all of the project being worked on with a tool or machine.